FOOTBALL FORFEITS

Fun activities, challenges and forfeits for football-mad kids and teenagers!

Football Forfeits:
Fun activities, challenges and forfeits for football-mad kids and teenagers.

© 2021, Zac Marks.
All Rights Reserved.

While every effort has been taken to ensure the safety and suitability of the activities and forfeits contained in this book, all participants (and their parents) must take responsibility for assessing levels of risk. The author and publisher accept no liability for damage or injury resulting from the use of this publication.

The fun starts here...

Ready to take some risks, face some challenges and have some fun?

This book contains some ideas for games you can play with your friends, along with some fun forfeits for the loser to enjoy!

It's the perfect game if you're meeting up with mates for the afternoon and looking for something different to do, or why not use it for a football-themed birthday party or a forfeit-filled sleepover? Or perhaps you need a fresh idea for your fundraiser or for your social media channel?

You might, of course, regret it when you have to clean your mate's football boots or do something even worse!

So, are you sure you're up for it? Really?

Then let's go!

Play nicely!

While you enjoy playing 'Football Forfeits' there are a couple of things you need to remember:

- **Don't fall out with your friends over this.** It's a game that's meant to be all about having fun. If someone really doesn't want to do something, don't try and make them! Agree in advance what your ground rules are, and which forfeits are in play. Don't be upset if you lose a challenge – try and enjoy it all as part of the game.

- **Check your parents are happy.** Make sure they know you are taking part, and if you plan on filming any of the challenges then do double-check with them before you upload anything to social media or anywhere else. And, of course, don't upload any videos of your friends without their permission.

- **Play safely.** The games and forfeits in this book are all pretty safe, but <u>everything you do is at your own risk</u>. If it's minus six degrees, don't pour water over your mate! If they're allergic to eggs, don't break one over them! Make sure your parents know what you're up to, and have agreed to it. Got it? Great!

Get your kit on!

'Football Forfeits' is designed for people to play while wearing football kit. That helps to get people in the zone but it's also because some of the forfeits will only work well if you are all properly kitted out for football!

That means:
- Football shirt / t-shirt
- Football shorts
- Long football socks (essential – but they don't need to be pulled up… yet!)
- Boots or trainers

If it's cold then you can also wear thermal or base layers under your kit, but that's entirely optional. Don't wear shin guards, but do have some to hand. Check out the next page for information on what else you'll need…

Get your bag packed!

You can play 'Football Forfeits' at home or at the park. It's entirely up to you, but if you're going to be able to do all of the forfeits you'll need to have these things to hand:

- A football (obviously!)
- A bottle of water for each player plus one extra
- A smartphone
- Shin guards (ideally one set per player)
- A spare pair of football socks or a school tie
- Shaving foam
- Hair gel or styling product
- A few eggs (packed carefully!)
- Some underpants (any style/colour – the more embarrassing the better)
- A spare t-shirt/top or two, one of which you or your friends would really not want to wear (maybe a vest or the football shirt of a team you/they hate? Or a school shirt? Or a top that your brother/sister is happy to lend?)

Some of the suggested rounds work better with goalposts. If you can play near a proper goal (or two) or have some small goals you can use then that would be ideal, but if that isn't possible you may want to mark some out with some spare water bottles, cones or other markers.

Using the forfeits...

If you're playing with friends, you need to agree how you're going to use the forfeits:

- You can use a free random number app on your phone to select a forfeit, or you can get someone who hasn't read the forfeits to choose a random number from 1 to 30.

- You need to decide whether you are you going to know what it is (and agree it) before you start to play or whether you are going to wait until someone loses before they find out what they have to do.

- If you are playing with more than two of you, is everyone except the winner going to do the forfeit, or only the person who comes last?

- If the same forfeit is chosen twice will you repeat it or choose a different one?

Double or nothing!

Each forfeit has a 'Double or Nothing' option.

The idea is that someone can try to escape from a forfeit by saying 'Double or Nothing'.

If they say that, and then they win the next round of the game, then they don't have to do the forfeit. But if they lose the next round then their forfeit gets even worse!

If a player chooses 'Double or Nothing' and loses the following round, <u>not only do they have to do the worse forfeit, but they also have to complete another forfeit for the round they just lost!</u>

You can choose to play 'Football Forfeits' without using the 'Double or Nothing' option if you'd prefer. Some of the 'Double' options are pretty severe, so make sure the person knows what they are agreeing to before they opt to use one!

An alternative way to use the 'Double or Nothing' forfeit is to use the 'Double' version if a player ends up with the same forfeit as they've had before.

THE GAMES

Round 1.
Beat the Goalie!

Practice those penalties!

This works best if you have some proper goals, but you can always improvise with some cones or water bottles.

If two of you are playing then each player takes a set number of penalties with the other player in goal. Then swap around. Whoever scores the most is the winner of the round.

If you draw then it's sudden death: one penalty each until one player scores and the other doesn't.

If more than two of you are playing then simply you all take turns, ensuring everyone gets the same number of penalties.

<u>*Try it with a twist!*</u>
Fancy testing your goalie skills instead of your penalty-taking abilities? One player goes in goal and the others all take three shots against them. Then swap over. Whoever saves the most goals wins!

Round 2.
One vs. One

It's time to get stuck in!

Set two drinking bottles up, one at either end of the pitch - the pitch size is entirely up to you – this can work just as well in a small space as a large one.

Place the ball right in the middle and then each player stands by their bottle.

On the count of three, the game starts. The aim is to knock over the other player's bottle with the ball. If you kick over the opponent's bottle, or accidently knock over your own bottle, then you lose!

If you have more than two players, you can hold a mini-tournament of one vs. one matches until everyone has played everyone else.

Round 3.
Kick It Up

Start simple!

Whoever can do the most kick-ups wins, and whoever does the least loses!

You might want to agree that each person gets at least five attempts at this, and that their best attempt is the one used as their final score.

Round 4.
Target Practice

Time to use those drinks bottles again, but this time for a bit of target practice!

Start with them a short distance away. Each player has to take a shot at them to knock them down. If they miss, they keep taking shots until they succeed. Every shot they take adds a point to their total.

Once everyone has succeeded in knocking the bottles down, they can be moved further away. You will need to agree before the round starts how many different distances you are going to try: three is suggested.

The person with the least points (who has taken the least shots) by the end of the round wins this round, and whoever took the most attempts loses.

Short on space?
Rather than increasing the distance, why not make everyone use their left foot (or their right foot if they normally use their left)? Or make them turn on the spot five times clockwise then anticlockwise before they take their shot!

Round 5.
Break a Sweat

Are you up for finding out who's fastest?

If you're in a large open space then place some cones or drinks bottles around to make a small circuit or obstacle course.

Use this course for three separate mini-rounds. The loser of each mini-round takes a forfeit:

- First, a simple speed test. Who can run the course the fastest without the ball?

- Second, a speed-skills test. Who can run the course the fastest with the ball? You may want to agree a time penalty if they kick the ball more than two metres away at any point!

- Third, an endurance test. Who can do the most laps of the course in a three-minute or five-minute period?

Round 6.
Attack and Defend

Time to get physical!

You need a small goal for this game, or to mark one out with two cones.

One player is the attacker and the other the defender. You play for five minutes, and the attacker needs to score as many goals as they can in the time available. Then the players swap around.

More people playing? Then play two vs. two or hold a mini-tournament.

Round 7.
Fetch!

This round will only work if you are in a really large open space such as a park.

You'll need a way of keeping time, such as a stopwatch on your phone.

One player boots the ball as far as they possibly can, and then starts the stopwatch. The other player has to run and fetch the ball back. They can kick or carry the ball back to the person who kicked it, but they have to tag them while holding the ball in order for the timer to be stopped.

Then the two players swap over. Whoever took the longest to fetch the ball loses.

If you are playing this game with more than two players then simply take turns in each of the roles.

THE FORFEITS

1. Lose the Shoes

Next time you're involved in a round that doesn't involve tackling other players, you have to do it without your boots or trainers.

Double or Nothing?
If you end up with 'Double' then you have to do all the remaining skills rounds (except those involving tackling other players) without your boots/trainers.

2. Push-ups

Drop and do twenty push-ups. If you fail or collapse then you have to do another forfeit!

Double or Nothing?
If you end up with 'Double' then you have to do fifty push-ups or you get another forfeit!

3. Wet Hair

The winner is allowed to pour some water over your head – not a whole bottle but enough to get you wet! You have to stand still and let them do it!

Double or Nothing?
If you end up with 'Double' then it happens after every round which you don't win, until you win one!

4. High Socks

Pull your football socks as high as they will go and keep them like that for an hour. If they drop below your knees then the other players can make you take another forfeit.

Double or Nothing?
If you end up with 'Double' then you have to wear your socks high for the rest of the day until bedtime!

5. Sit-ups

Do twenty-five sit-ups with your hands crossed over your chest. If you fail to complete them without a rest then you have to take another forfeit.

Double or Nothing?
If you end up with 'Double' then you have to do fifty sit-ups without pausing, or take another forfeit.

6. Kiss

Don't panic! You don't have to kiss the winner or anyone else on the lips. But you do need to kneel down and kiss the winner's boots!

Double or Nothing?
If you end up with 'Double' then you have to do this to the winner of every round from now on, even if you don't come last!

7. Shin Guards

Time to put on your shin-guards under your football socks! You have to wear them for at least an hour.

Double or Nothing?
If you end up with 'Double' then you have to keep them on until bedtime!

8. Fitness Coach

The winner gets to be your fitness coach for the next five minutes! Whatever they do, you have to do triple! So, if they do ten press-ups, you do thirty! If they do one lap of the pitch, you have to do three! If you can't hack it then you'll need to do another forfeit!

Double or Nothing?
If you end up with 'Double' then your fitness session lasts for ten minutes and you have to do four times the amount of any exercise they do! Enjoy!

9. Sing

You have to sing something for the other players. You get to choose the song – it could be something in the charts, or it could be a nursery rhyme. But sing away!

Double or Nothing?
If you end up with 'Double' then you have to dance along as you sing!

10. Underpants

You have to put an embarrassing pair of underpants on over your football shorts! It stays on for the next round.

Double or Nothing?
If you end up with 'Double' then you keep the pants on for the next two hours!

11. Yes Sir!

You have to call the other players 'Sir' or 'Ma'am' until you next win a round. If you're caught using anyone's name then you have to take another forfeit!

Double or Nothing?
If you end up with 'Double' then you have to keep on calling the others 'Sir' or 'Ma'am' for the rest of the day, even if you win a round!

12. Kit Kid

You have to stay in your football kit until bedtime! This includes everything you're wearing by the time you finish playing the game!

Double or Nothing?
If you end up with 'Double' then you even get to sleep in it all! Let's hope that doesn't include shin guards...

13. Burpees

Do twenty burpees.

A burpee involves repeating the following movements: Crouch down. Then put your hands on the ground and jump back with your legs until you are in the push-up position. Now jump forward with your legs so you're back where you started. Now stand up, put your hands high in the air and jump as high as you can. Do it fast and that's one burpee!

Double or Nothing?
If you end up with 'Double' then you have to do forty burpees! That's going to hurt...

14. Phoneless

You can't use your phone for an hour, unless your parents text or ring!

Double or Nothing?
If you end up with 'Double' then you lose phone privileges for two hours. Unlucky!

15. Dirty Boots

You get to clean the winner's football boots – they can cash this in whenever they like!

Double or Nothing?
If you end up with 'Double' then you have to clean the boots of everyone else playing as well. If you are only playing one other person, then they can make you clean their boots on two different occasions!

16. Rambo

Use a spare football sock or school tie, and wrap it around your head like a headband! It has to stay there for at least an hour!

Double or Nothing?
If you end up with 'Double' then you have to wear the headband for as long as the other players demand it, so probably until bedtime!

17. Balance

Stand on one leg for three minutes. Once you've started, you can't change legs. If you put your other foot down then you have to take another forfeit.

Double or Nothing?
If you end up with 'Double' then you have to do it with your eyes closed. Fail and it's another forfeit I'm afraid!

18. Top Forfeit

The winner can choose a new top for you to wear. Yes, even the sweaty football shirt they're currently wearing! Or something worse... You have to keep it on until you win a round.

Double or Nothing?
If you end up with 'Double' then you have to keep the top on until bedtime, even if you win a round!

19. Gunge

The winner decides what you have to put in your pants. It could be dried grass, leaves, mud or shaving foam (but it can't be an egg). You can't take the stuff out!

Double or Nothing?
If you end up with 'Double' then they can also put stuff down your shirt and football socks as well – it's basically a full gunging (still, no eggs though – that's a different forfeit).

20. Fashion Sense

Tuck your shirt in and pull your shorts up as high as they will go. They have to stay like that until you win a round.

Double or Nothing?
If you end up with 'Double' then you have to stay like that until bedtime!

21. Plank

Hold the plank position for at least two minutes. If you fail then take another forfeit.

The plank is a bit like the way you start a push-up, except your arms are bent and your forearms rest on the ground. You have to keep your body straight and knees off the ground and stay still throughout.

Double or Nothing?
If you end up with 'Double' then you have to manage three whole minutes or take another forfeit.

22. Choice

The winner can choose any forfeit from this book for you to do!

Double or Nothing?
If you end up with 'Double' then the winner gets to choose two forfeits for you from this book!

23. Apology

Post an apology to the winner on social media. Say sorry for wasting their time when they are clearly so much better at football than you are. You have to leave it there for at least 24 hours!

Double or Nothing?
If you end up with 'Double' then you could film yourself actually saying the apology to the camera and then post it for added effect! Then leave it there for a week!

24. Run, Run, Run

You have to run non-stop for two minutes. If you stop then you have to take another forfeit.

Double or Nothing?
If you end up with 'Double' then you have to run non-stop for four minutes, or take another forfeit.

25. Wet Clothes

Pour some water in your pants so it looks like you've had an accident!

Double or Nothing?
If you end up with 'Double' then the winner gets to empty a water bottle over you – shirt, shorts, socks, wherever they like! Stand still and let them do it!

26. Hairstyle

The winner can style your hair using water or hair gel in any way they want. You have to leave it like that for at least an hour!

Double or Nothing?
If you end up with 'Double' then you have to leave your hair like that until bedtime!

27. Human Target

Stand up and bend over, facing away from the winner. They get to blast the ball at your backside from five metres away. They get five shots.

Double or Nothing?
If you end up with 'Double' then the winner gets ten shots at you!

28. Eggs

The winner gets to crack an egg over your head.

Double or Nothing?
If you end up with 'Double' then the winner gets to crack two eggs over you – one on your head, and another down your pants! And no, you can't remove any of it!

29. Servant

The winner can ask you to fetch and carry their stuff for the next hour – get them drinks, etc.

Double or Nothing?
If you end up with 'Double' then you're their personal servant for the rest of the day! That means they could even make you clean their bedroom…

30. Fill Your Boots!

The winner gets to fill your boots or trainers with shaving foam (or water). Then you have to put them on!

Double or Nothing?
If you end up with 'Double' then they also get to fill their hands with shaving foam and rub it in your face and hair!

Get Xtreme!

Wait!? What? You want even more forfeit ideas? Are you nuts? Well, the great news is that you can download some more extreme forfeit ideas <u>completely free</u>!

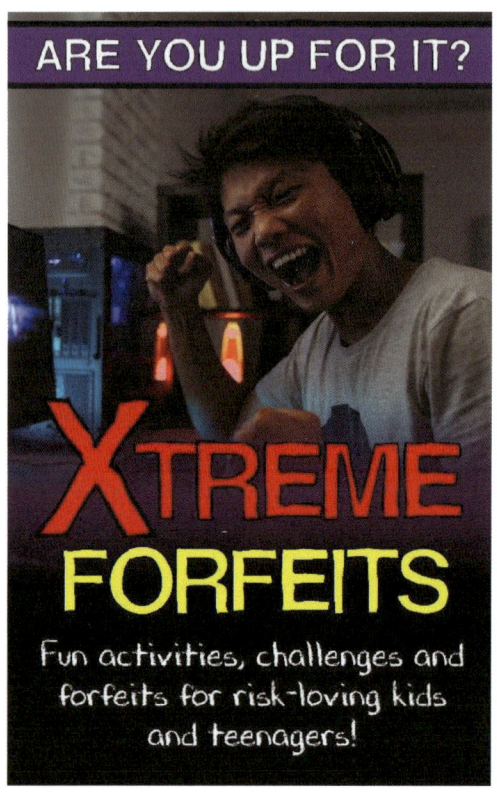

GET YOUR FREE DOWNLOAD

Visit: rotf.lol/xtremeforfeits

Share the madness...

Want to connect with others on Instagram or Youtube?

Use the following hashtag:

#funforfeitsbooks

And on Instagram, tag me, the author:

@ZacMarksAuthor

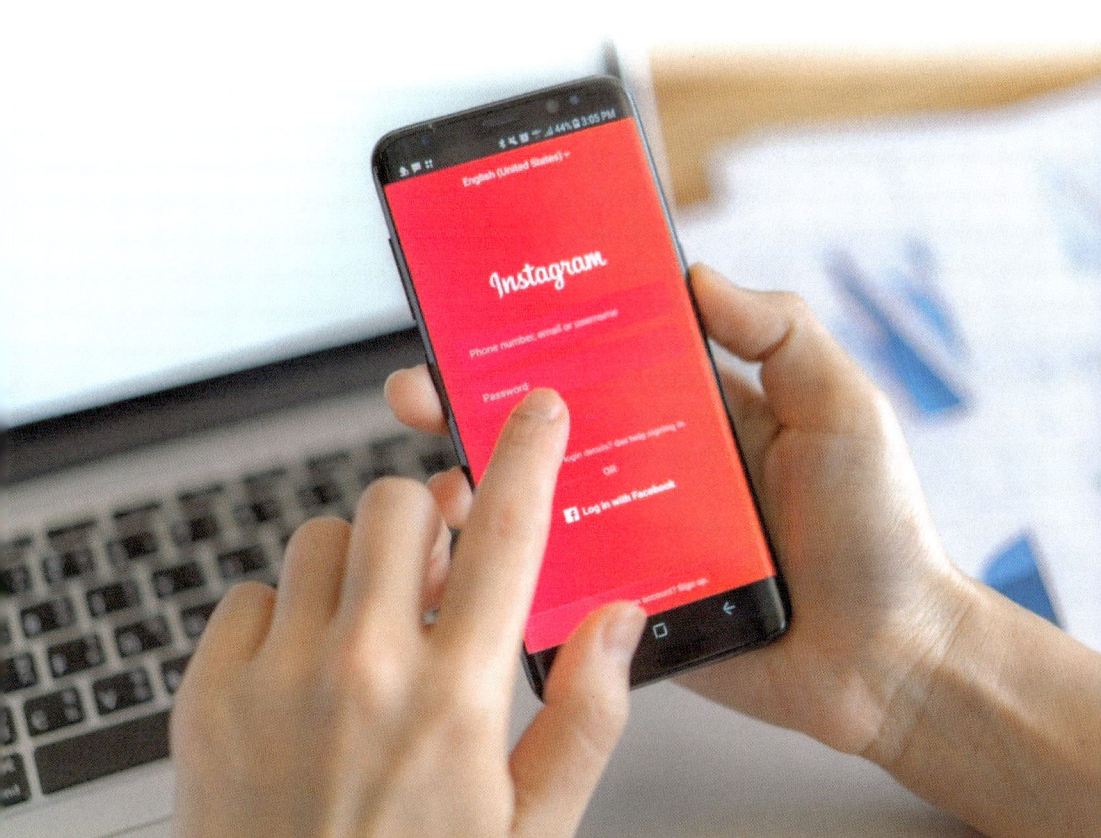

One last thing

Thanks for buying 'Football Forfeits' – I hope it's given you loads of ideas for some great challenges with your friends!

If you've enjoyed it then please do leave a positive review on Amazon. It's really helpful for others, and I love to know what people *really* think about what I write.

Don't forget to download 'Xtreme Forfeits' for free if you want some more crazy ideas! That way I can also let you know about any new books, freebies or special offers you might be interested in.

You can get your free download at **rotf.lol/xtremeforfeits**

In the meantime, if you want to get in touch with me then you can e-mail me at:

zacmarks@gmx.co.uk

Whatever you do, keep playing and laughing, and making your friends suffer...

All the best,

Zac.

Printed in Great Britain
by Amazon